SAFETY ON THE HILLS

(In this pamphlet the term *Scouts* is used to denote all members and Sections of the Movement).

INTRODUCTION

Scouting has for a long time aimed to develop an awareness of nature in young people through camping, adventurous activities and exploring.

For older Scouts, particular emphasis is given to adventure in moorland and mountain areas which are potentially hazardous. This demands from their Leaders a whole range of technical skills without which they cannot make those necessary decisions forced upon them in these situations.

Over the past years some Scouts have been injured and a few have died in the mountains. Leaders need to realise the responsibilities involved when leading parties in potentially hazardous country and to take training so as to acquire the necessary experience and skills.

The Leader of a party of Scouts is responsible for their safety and in this he has the parents' trust and confidence. For this purpose The Hill Safety Code has been written. It is for general application and compliance by all members of the Movement engaged in any hill activity, and includes the preparation and the actual carrying out of the planned activity.

The main reason for hill walking accidents is underestimation of the "small" but dangerous hills of Britain and their associated weather conditions, and inadequate preparation, training and equipment.

Lack of preparation and training could result in losing the way, which always wastes valuable time. This gives bad weather and darkness an opportunity to weaken, and perhaps destroy, through exposure, the badly equipped and ill-led party. A party in that state is in great danger from exposure in wet and cold conditions, and if that party splits up during the night, by morning those who have not found shelter may well be lost and exhausted, alone in a barren wilderness facing the real possibility of death from exposure, unless help comes. Others may be DEAD already.

TRAINING

To ensure responsible leadership, suitable training of Leaders and Instructors is necessary. Such training is being incorporated in all appropriate Basic and Advanced Leader Training Courses. Similar training along these lines is also necessary for Scouts. Counties and Districts must be aware of the need for Leaders to gain experience in the five fields below if they intend to undertake these activities.

Scout Leaders should lead or authorise expeditions only if competent and when given approval to do so. Where possible every encouragement should be given for Scouters to train for the Mountain Leadership Certificate (see page 17).

EXPERIENCE

No Leader should take or be responsible for Scouts, in any of the three areas where these Rules apply (see next section), if he has not had the following minimum experience:

1. He should have acquired and studied the Mountain Rescue Committee's handbook *Mountain Rescue and Cave Rescue* and The Sports Council's *Safety on Mountains*.
2. Ideally he should have climbed at least ten different hills over 600 metres (2,000ft.), preferably during at least two years, of which one week could be said to be under some form of instruction – from experienced friends; from guides; on The Sports Council's or climbing school course; or on climbing club meets for beginners. The areas intended for Scout activities should be of a standard well within this experience.
3. He should have had previous experience and have understanding of the conditions likely to be encountered, especially cold, mist, rain, high winds, ice and snow. Quickly worsening weather,

particularly in Scotland, and innocent looking ice and snow on beaten tracks at Christmas and Easter are among the most lethal of all the conditions likely to be experienced.

4. He must be competent in the use of map and compass in rain, mist and bad weather conditions in the mountains. Route planning and navigation skills are amongst the most important for competent leadership in the mountains.
5. He must have a knowledge of the problems of Hypothermia (Exposure), must be able to take action to prevent it, and be able to recognise the signs and know the treatment. He must also have a knowledge of First Aid relevant to mountain situations.

The Syllabus of training for the Mountain Leadership Certificate, given in more detail in Appendix B, gives the main areas of skill required, i.e.:

1. Map and compass navigation;
2. Route planning – including escape routes;
3. Walking skills;
4. Personal equipment;
5. Camping equipment;
6. Campcraft;
7. Security on steep ground (elementary ropework);
8. River crossing;
9. Special mountain hazards (e.g. hypothermia);
10. Weather;
11. Accident procedure;
12. Details of clubs, organisations, etc.;
13. Responsibilities of Party Leader, etc.;
14. Additional interests.

These are the minimum requirements and no-one should ignore the benefit to be derived from increased experience and more advanced training, training in First Aid being essential before the Mountain Leadership Certificate is awarded.

APPLICATION

It is clearly important that all Leaders understand the application of the relevant parts of *Policy, Organisation and Rules* and the Hill Safety Code. They both apply in three distinct areas:

(a) To those parties in areas usually below 600 metres (2,000ft.), not covered in section (b) below, that offer little protection against wind/rain/cold/snow under inclement weather conditions.

Leaders must ensure that *Scout* parties in these areas, which include the Fens, Downs, Wolds, Hills, Plains, Moors, Heaths, Forests and waste land, are equipped as for the more obviously 'potentially hazardous' country described in (b) below when the weather conditions and/or the time of year make this necessary.

(b) To those parties in the following areas where bad weather is normal, and good weather the exception:

Dartmoor; Exmoor; Bodmin Moor;
the Peak District; the Pennines;
the Cheviot Hills;
the North Yorkshire Moors;
the Cumbrian Mountains of the Lake District;
the Cambrian Mountains – Snowdonia and North Wales generally; Mid Wales; South Wales – Brecon Beacons and Black Mountains.

The Isle of Man.

Scotland – the Southern Uplands, the Grampians and the North-West Highlands, the Inner and Outer Hebrides, Orkney and Shetland.

Ireland – the Sperrin Mountains, and North Antrim Hills, Mourne Mountains, and those other areas termed Mountains in the Irish Republic.

Other similar areas not defined above also qualify under this heading.

(c) To those parties on hill/mountaineering expeditions abroad. In these cases The Hill Safety Code needs to be augmented by considerably more experience and training, especially in snow/ice techniques, and the use of local and/or professional guides should be carefully considered.

Costs of Mountain Rescue are very high and enquiries should be made of The British Mountaineering Council, Room 314, Third Floor, 26 Park Crescent, London W1N 4EE for details of Mountain Rescue Insurance Schemes that may be available in any particular year.

SUMMARY

It is The Scout Association's policy to prevent avoidable accidents in the hills by training Leaders; by giving positive guidance on the basic precautions necessary for safety on the hills; and by arrangements for accidents and reports of dangerous occurrences to Scouts to be investigated.

The instructions and procedures for safety on the hills, with which every Leader must be familiar, form a code of good practice similar to the Highway Code. The rules in the Highway Code can be broken, but when this leads to an accident blame is not easily avoided.

Safety on the hills is exactly the same and neglect of the standards it sets make accidents more likely to happen. At an enquiry into an accident or a dangerous occurrence the Leader must be prepared to explain why he followed, if necessary, a chosen course of action which might have been in breach of the guidance in *Safety on the Hills*.

Proper care and responsibility for others, together with suitable training for all concerned should greatly reduce the risk of accidents. In this way Scouts can enjoy unhindered the opportunities for adventure that are to be found in adventurous country.

NOTES

(a) It is strongly recommended that those leading or authorising activities in potentially hazardous or unknown country should seek advice from a Mountaineering Adviser (see paragraph 40(ii) on page 23. A leaflet defining the role of the Mountaineering Adviser is available from Scout Headquarters. Advisers are appointed locally and not by Headquarters.

(b) The duties of Commissioners and Leaders in ensuring the safety of Scouts in all circumstances are given, starting on page 19.

(c) All Leaders concerned with taking *Scouts* to wild and potentially hazardous country are strongly recommended to gain the Mountain Leadership Certificate.

THE HILL SAFETY CODE

The Hill Safety Code states the minimum precautions that are necessary. Its instructions will be followed by all Scouts. A Leader who departs from these must be prepared to explain, if necessary, why he chose to do so. (Note: For Skiers only. The instructions may be relaxed at the discretion of the party leader while they are ski-ing in the vicinity of an established ski piste or a working public chair-lift or tow).

While what follows must be adhered to, in addition to this experience, understanding and training is necessary to be able to use the equipment mentioned.

A - GETTING READY

(a) Plan for bad weather, which is normal in potentially hazardous country.

(b) Leader must be able to use map and compass, accurately and in mist.

(c) Prepare a detailed route card showing distances to be covered and height to be climbed. Naismith's Rule gives a *guide* for timing routes but may need to be modified further depending on the abilities of the party:

> $2\frac{1}{2}$ miles per hour and 1 hour for 450 metres (1,500ft.) of ascent.
>
> 2 miles per hour and 1 hour for 300 metres (1,000ft.) of ascent if laden.

(d) Plan for the slowest member of the party. Time and plan interesting and enjoyable routes carefully, allowing many spare hours in relation to the amount of daylight.

(e) Plan an alternative bad weather low-level route.

(f) Note clearly defined escape routes for all stages of the journey.

(g) Leave with a responsible person (probably 'The Communicator' – see *Policy, Organisation and Rules*, Appendix VIII Rule 39(iii)) or Mountain Rescue Post, a copy of the route card and your estimated time of return and inform those concerned on return or arrival in safe country. Check the local methods of leaving routes (in Wales, leaving a message with Mountain Rescue Posts for instance; in Scotland, the note-on-the-car-seat is much more frequently used).

(h) Know the Mountain Rescue Posts and teams of the area.

(i) Be weatherwise. Remember that the weather can change very quickly; if conditions are bad in the valley they will be considerably worse higher up and a walk which was found easy in summer may be very different in winter. Always plan your route in relation to the prevailing conditions, and be very cautious about what you attempt in bad weather.

B - SIZE OF PARTY

No expedition in potentially hazardous country should be undertaken by a party of less than four, although in exceptional circumstances this may be reduced to three. Never go alone or in pairs. Ten, including two experienced leaders, is the maximum party size and this is only advisable with low-level journeys.

With larger numbers, form separate parties each with adequate, experienced and trained leadership.

For higher and/or longer and/or snow/ice type expeditions six is the optimum number, and it is recommended that two experienced Leaders are included.

C - EQUIPMENT

Equipment is important. The further and higher you go the better the equipment needed. The following are lists of the minimum personal and party equipment.

List (i) has been prepared for hill walking in summer.

List (ii). In winter, snow/ice work and climbing should be expected and additional equipment is necessary.

List (iii). Any journeys which are long and/or

high-level require additional basic equipment.

ROCK CLIMBING requires further equipment (ropes, karabiners, helmets, etc.). When rock climbing a party must be in the charge of a leader with recent experience of rock climbs of comparable standard. On single-pitch outcrops the maximum is six persons to one instructor and second, and on multi-pitch climbs the maximum is three persons on a rope. The leader must climb well within his standard, and realise that with beginners on the rope he is virtually climbing solo.

SKI-ING needs its own special equipment.

(i) *Summer weather conditions – PERSONAL KIT to be* **worn/carried** *by* **each person.** *Brightly coloured (orange) clothing is always recommended.*

Waterproof outer garment above and below the waist – Helly-Hansen recommended. An improvised waterproof outer 'shell' is a large 500 or 1,000 gauge polythene bag with face hole. A windproof anorak with hood or long windproof jacket with hood may be worn provided additional waterproofs as above are taken.

Balaclava and gloves/mitts.

Warm trousers or breeches – shorts and jeans should not be worn as they give little protection from rain and strong wind and so are liable to lead to exposure.

Warm long-sleeved shirt, underwear (string vest), thick woollen socks.

Long sleeved pullover – and spare in rucsac.

Strong boots with Vibram or Commando Soles designed for mountain use. Avoid footwear with smooth or near-smooth soles.

Food for the day.

Emergency food – 4 oz. chocolate, mint cake, glucose tablets.

Rucsac: one per three people.

Whistle.

Torch: at least two 2-3 U2 battery size torches, with spare batteries and bulbs.

PARTY KIT

Compass: at least two per party – Silva type recommended.

Map of area: at least two suitable O.S. Maps 1:63,360 (1:50,000) or 1:25,000 per party.

* First Aid Kit.

Man-sized polythene survival bag – 500 or 1,000 gauge. $2\frac{2}{3}$ x $1\frac{1}{3}$ metres (8ft. x 4ft.) for use in cases of exposure — at least one.

Rope: 40 metres (120ft.) No. 2, 3 or 4 nylon rope – for use where unexpected route difficulties are met.

* First Aid Kit. This should contain as a minimum:

Plasters (for blisters and cuts); lint or gauze (for dressings, etc.); Acriflavine Cream (antiseptic and soothing cream, useful for burns. cuts, etc.); Aspirin, etc. (for headaches and pain), a selection of bandages, an 8cm. (3in.) crepe bandage (for strains), a triangular bandage, scissors, pencil and paper.

Salt tablets are a very useful commodity in mountains and may sometimes relieve cramp.

(ii) *Winter Conditions.*

All the equipment in List (i) is required;

In addition:

Spare polythene survival bag.

Down sleeping bag.

Stove and equipment for hot drink/thermos between three; and the necessary food.

Ice-axe per person and training in ice-axe techniques.

Crampons for the Leader.

Rope – (see i) – one between three.

(iii) *Long and/or High Level Journeys.*

All the equipment in List (i) is required.

In addition:

Winter conditions equipment (ii) during winter.

Equipment to deal with exposure and/or an overnight camp – e.g. tents.

Additional waterproof equipment.

In potentially hazardous country during periods of heavy rain, strong winds and low temperatures people have died from hypothermia (exposure).

THESE PEOPLE MIGHT NOT HAVE DIED IF THEY HAD NOT BEEN WET THROUGH – GOOD EQUIPMENT IS ESSENTIAL.

D - ON THE HILL

(a) Watch the *weather* constantly. On high ground mist, rain or snow can close in with alarming speed.
(b) Do not be afraid to abandon the journey via an *escape route*.
(c) Leader chooses *route* and *sets* pace which is that of the slowest walker, and appoints rear man to keep party together, ensuring that all members of the party have adequate rests.
(d) Wait after *obstacles* for party to re-form.
(e) Do not split the party except in an emergency.
(f) Watch for signs of *exhaustion* or hypothermia (exposure). Know the *causes* and treatment for hypothermia.
(g) Know the correct procedure for dealing with an *accident* – (see page 13). Have a plan in mind for taking shelter if necessary in bad weather or darkness.
(h) Do not leave *rucsacs* behind when making a detour to an outlying peak.
(i) If for any reason you do not return to your base as planned, as soon as possible after you are off the hill tell your base or the *police* by message or 'phone what has happened. Failure to do this promptly may cause search parties to waste time looking for you.
(j) *Whistles, flares, shouting, torches,* etc., should only be used in emergencies and not for wide-games, etc.
(k) Keep track of the *time* and *distance* covered so that you always know where you are. Do not hesitate to *turn back* if the weather breaks or the route is too much for any of the party, or if you cannot complete the planned route before darkness. 'Pressing on' is *folly,* not pluck, and can be disastrous.
(l) Keep off ice, and away from snow slopes and cornices *until* you have learned the techniques necessary for safe ski-ing or snow and ice climbing. Do *not* attempt any type of ice or rock climbing without proper training and equipment.

(m) — see top of page 9 for rock climbing.

(n) Above all the party must keep together and accept all decisions by the Leader. To leave a straggler behind can be to sentence him to death.

E - HYPOTHERMIA/EXPOSURE, OR WET/COLD EXHAUSTION

Collapse and possible death from exposure is brought on by the failure of the person to maintain body core temperature either by keeping himself dry or by maintaining a high work output, with its accompanying warming effect. Consequently, it should be appreciated that a tired, frightened or hungry walker, carrying even a light load who is wet and cold through to the skin is a possible victim of exposure, especially if the apparent air temperature should fall to near zero centigrade, through the effects of wind.

Signs and Symptoms

It is not easy to recognise a mild case of exposure in a party, and yet it is extremely important that the signs of a *Scout* approaching a crisis are not overlooked. The following are among the most usual symptoms, of which one or more may be present:

(a) A slowing of the rate of progress with complaints about coldness and tiredness.

(b) Clumsiness and stumbling, with failure to respond to simple directions, and mental lethargy.

(c) Disturbance of speech and/or vision.

(d) Sudden shivering fits.

(e) Collapse.

(f) Irrational or unreasonable behaviour.

(g) Argumentative: sudden bursts of energy.

In view of the relatively short period of time (between 1 and 2 hours) between the onset of the symptoms and collapse it is essential that urgent and correct action is taken.

The condition of the Scout must not be allowed to deteriorate further, and this means that pressing on is NOT the answer, unless shelter is only *minutes* away. Once the victim is only capable of low level physical activity the time has come to STOP and make some sort of camp on the spot. If possible a tent should be erected; failing this anoraks and poly-bags, etc., must be made into a bivouac.

Treatment

The following treatment should then be given:

(a) *STOP AT ONCE.* Do not allow serious disability or collapse to develop. See Accident Procedure, below, for details on sending for help.

(b) Insulate the victim against further heat loss, i.e. put him into a man-sized polythene survival bag, with further padding underneath it. If possible place another fit climber in with the victim or close alongside for warmth. Make the whole set-up as windproof as possible.

(c) Give the victim food – condensed milk and hot drinks if a stove or thermos are available. A stove will also heat the inside of the tent, if in use.

(d) Reassure the patient – fear greatly accelerates exhaustion.

(e) Follow ACCIDENT PROCEDURE: see below.

This treatment is directed at (1) preventing further loss of body heat and (2) raising the body core temperature. NO ATTEMPT EITHER BY RUBBING, HOT WATER BOTTLES OR ALCOHOL SHOULD BE MADE TO WARM THE SKIN OF THE VICTIM; this would only cause a rush of blood to the skin and further core cooling.

When the stretcher party arrives all the insulation around the victim should be preserved during the carry.

On arrival at base

If possible the best treatment, preferably carried out with a doctor present, is rapid rewarming in a warm bath – not to exceed 45°C i.e. the hottest temperature in which a bare elbow can be *kept*. When the patient begins to sweat he can be removed to a warm room (21°C) until the doctor decides that he is out of danger.

F - ACCIDENT PROCEDURE

Don't rush. Keep calm.

Take immediate action to avoid another accident.

Assess injury.

If necessary – restart victim's breathing using artificial resuscitation.

Stop serious bleeding.

Protect victim from the weather (polythene survival bag).
Reassure victim and treat for shock.
Deal with fractures.

Send two competent messengers (*one* if only three in party), to make a 999 call for help from the nearest telephone, by a safe route. The attention of the messengers is drawn to the "Immediate Action" section of Appendix A, ACCIDENT PROCEDURES AND REPORTS, see page 24.

They should have a written message which should include:

Six figure map reference, name and description of site of accident;
time of accident;
number of people involved;
extent of injuries.

While waiting for help employ the rest of the party with simple tasks to keep up their morale, e.g. build shelter round injured, brew up, etc. Watch for signs of hypothermia in rest of the party. Try and make your position conspicuous from a distance by improvising a flag, whistling, etc.

Attempt to attract local help

Give the International Alpine Distress Signal – six successive long blasts on a whistle, or flashes, followed by a minute's silence and a repeat of six blasts – this to continue until help is attracted. The acknowledgement signal consists of three blasts in a minute followed by a minute's silence, then repeated.

G - MOUNTAIN RESCUE SIGNAL CODE

Signals by pyrotechnic (flares) are often used on search or rescue operations and walkers should be aware of what they mean. The Mountain Rescue Committee have agreed on a standard form, which is as follows:

Red flares are used to indicate 'position of the accident' or 'I require aid'.

White flares are used to indicate an acknowledgement.

Green flares are used to recall to base, as are a succession of notes on horn, bell or whistle, thunderflashes or lights switched on and off.

NO OTHER USE OF PYROTECHNIC SIGNALS (FLARES) IS JUSTIFIED, without prior notification to all those in the district involved in mountain rescue – see the current booklet of the Mountain Rescue Committee. If a party is fully trained, equipped and briefed taking *MINIFLARES* is to be recommended.

H - PUBLICITY

Public Relations may not appear to be important at the time of an accident or incident, but inaccurate and misleading Press reports can cause a great deal of harm.

It is essential that a brief factual report be telephoned immediately to Scout Headquarters in London so that accurate information can be given to any Press enquiries. Leaders should telephone the Publicity Department, 01-834 6005. After hours: Harold Wyld, Barming Heath (Kent) 2244 or Jack Olden, 01-953 1393.

In Scotland: Office hours, Scottish Headquarters 031-226 7375. After hours: 031-332 5348.

I - FURTHER INFORMATION

Book List

The books given below all add much advice and guidance to the information in this leaflet. All Leaders must be conversant with 'SAFETY ON MOUNTAINS' and 'MOUNTAIN RESCUE AND CAVE RESCUE', and 'MOUNTAINEERING' is excellent as a standard reference book.

Safety on Mountains (The Sports Council; 48pp; 18p).

Mountaineering by Alan Blackshaw (Penguin; 542pp; £1.25).

Mountain Rescue and Cave Rescue (Mountain Rescue Committee; 68pp; 25p).

Mountain Rescue (H.M.S.O.; 178pp; 75p).

Mountain Leadership by Eric Langmuir (The Sports Council for Scotland, 89pp; 50p). Authorative and highly recommended.

Mountain Code (The Sports Council), 10 copies or more 2p each.

Mountain Safety Leaflet published by The Climber and Rambler.

Mountain Hypothermia (British Mountaineering Council; 5p).

Accident Procedure – card published by Ice Axes, Glencoe, Argyll, Scotland.

All the above are available either from or through the Equipment Department, Churchill Industrial Estate, Lancing, Sussex, or The Scottish Scout Shop, 39 and 43 Forrest Road, Edinburgh, EH1 2QU, or local suppliers. In case of difficulty the various Mountain Leadership Training Boards should be contacted (see page 17).

Reprints from SCOUTING magazine, safety posters, guidebooks, films, slides and general literature.

– a detailed leaflet is available from the Programme and Training Department, The Scout Association, 25 Buckingham Palace Road, London, SW1W OPY – please enclose stamped, addressed envelope.

Checklist of Skills based on the Mountain Leadership Course Syllabus (see Venture Scout Supplement, MAY 1972 issue of 'SCOUTING') – this is now available as a hand-out from Gilwell Park, Chingford, London, E4 7QW, price 1p each, excluding postage, or in bulk.

Explorer Films – a leaflet giving details of these documentary films on hill walking is also available from Gilwell Park, price 1p each, excluding postage.

The British Mountaineering Council run an Information Service. For full details, contact the B.M.C. – their address is on page 5.

J - MOUNTAIN LEADERSHIP TRAINING BOARD

In conjunction with The Sports Council the Board provides a comprehensive scheme of training for Leaders and Instructors in all aspects of mountaineering. In Scotland, the Scottish Mountain Leadership Training Board and the Sports Council for Scotland are responsible.

The Mountain Leadership Training Board operates the Mountain Leadership Certificate in England and Wales, and the equivalent in Scotland; the Scottish Mountain Leadership Summer Certificate is operated by the Scottish Mountain Leadership Training Board. It is recommended that all Leaders and Instructors either obtain or start working towards these Certificates which represent the *minimum* standards desirable. See Appendix B for the syllabus.

Certificates are gained in four stages:

1. A week of Basic Training.
2. Practical experience of at least a year.
3. Finally a week's Assessment Course.
4. A valid First-Aid Certificate is also needed for the award of the Mountain Leadership Certificate.

Exemption from the first two stages can be given to sufficiently experienced Leaders.

The various training Boards also operate the Mountaineering Instructor's Certificate and the Mountaineering Instructor's Advanced Certificate. The Scottish Mountain Leadership Training Board also operates the Winter Mountain Leadership Certificate.

Further information on any of the above Certificates from: The Secretary, Mountain Leadership Training Board, c/o The British Mountaineering Council, Room 314, Third Floor, 26 Park Crescent, London W1N 4EE.

The Secretary, Scottish Mountain Leadership Training Board, c/o The Sports Council for Scotland, 4, Queensferry Street, Edinburgh, EH2 4PB.

The Secretary, Northern Ireland Mountain Leadership Training Board, c/o Northern Ireland Youth and Sports Council, 49, Malone Road, Belfast, BT9 6RZ.

K - BURSARIES

Grants are generally available from Local Education Authorities who should always be approached.

In Scotland, the MacRobert Fund can help candidates with their course fees. Leave of absence can often be obtained from employers and is arranged through County Commissioners.

In other parts of the country help is available for leaders working towards the Winter Mountain Leadership Certificate, the Mountaineering Instructor's Certificate and the Mountaineering Instructor's Advanced Certificate. Further details of this Bursary are available from the Programme and Training Department, The Scout Association, 25 Buckingham Palace Road, London SW1W 0PY.

An extract from Policy, Organisation and Rules Parts I, II and III—Appendix VIII (Activities, Rules and Instructions)

ACTIVITIES IN POTENTIALLY HAZARDOUS COUNTRY

PREAMBLE

The Scout Association's programme encourages outdoor activities which are potentially hazardous, and this places a heavy responsibility upon those who authorise, train or lead parties in these pursuits.

This is inevitable, yet with careful planning, adequate training and expert advice the calculated risks can be minimised and more young people can enjoy, in greater safety, the challenge of this type of environment and in their turn help others to derive the same benefits.

The rules which follow must be read, interpreted and applied in conjunction with the more detailed advice and guidance contained in the Association's pamphlet 'Safety on the Hills'. Both these rules and the supporting guidance are designed to remind Leaders of their responsibilities:

(i) before undertaking such activities;
(ii) when giving instruction in the activity;
(iii) during the actual conduct of the activity;
(iv) in the event of an accident or emergency.

The appointment of qualified and experienced Mountaineering Advisers at County and District level to advise Commissioners and Leaders is a matter of priority. They should either hold, or have the equivalent experience of, the Mountain Leadership Certificate and take a major part in the provision and encouragement of skill training relating to activities in potentially hazardous country.

Finally, every Leader, however well trained and experienced, will inevitably face unforeseen situations. Here, he has not only responsibility for himself, but for the party he leads. He should avoid leading that party into circumstances of which he has not had prior personal experience. In particular he should not hesitate to return to a safer position if the situation demands.

38. Authorisation of Leadership

(i) No *Scout* shall take part in any activity in potentially hazardous country unless he has received proper training, is suitably equipped and briefed for the nature and scope of the activity, is of an appropriate age and is subject to authorised leadership;

(ii) The authorisation of leadership is normally the responsibility of the District Commissioner, but for particular events this authorisation may be granted by a Headquarters or County Commissioner;

(iii) (a) A Commissioner granting such authorisation must be satisfied that the individual concerned is qualified in that

Either (1) He holds the Winter Mountain Leadership Certificate;

or (2) He holds the Summer Mountain Leadership Certificate. For winter activities he has, in addition, sufficient experience of winter conditions to be able to lead in those conditions;

or (3) He satisfies a National, County or District Mountaineering Adviser that he possesses the necessary experience to ensure that the party is properly trained, equipped, briefed and led for the type of activity being authorised;

(b) Should it be impracticable for a Leader to qualify under the foregoing alternatives a Commissioner may grant authorisation for activities within prescribed limits and areas. In so doing he must have regard to the standards of qualification implicit in those alternatives and must be satisfied that the Leader possesses the necessary experience to ensure that the party is properly trained, equipped, briefed and led for the type of activity being authorised. If the Commissioner does not possess the required personal knowledge to carry out this duty he must seek advice from a suitable qualified person;

(iv) (a) Any Leader, Instructor or Venture Scout over 18 years of age authorised to lead by the foregoing rules may – *subject to prior agreement with the authorising Commissioner* – delegate responsibility to a Leader, Instructor, Venture Scout or Scout to lead and exercise full control over parties of Venture Scouts and Scouts *during* an expedition if it forms part of a properly planned training programme. This delegation should only be made to those who have sufficient training, experience and maturity of judgement to exercise responsible leadership in the anticipated conditions;

(b) Cub Scout parties may only be led by Leaders, Instructors or Venture Scouts over the age of 18 qualifying under rules (iii) (a) and (b).

39. Planning and Leading Expeditions

(i) Before undertaking any expedition in potentially hazardous country the authorised leader should ensure that all aspects of 'The Hill Safety Code' shown in the Association's pamphlet *Safety on the Hills;* and paragraph 39 (ii), are understood and, as applicable, are implemented;

(ii) Before giving permission to a *Scout* to take part in an activity in potentially hazardous country, it is the responsibility of the Leader or other person in charge to:–

(a) Seek up-to-date local and specialist information relating to the particular area and activity;

(b) Check that the training and equipment is followed in the event of an emergency;

(c) Consider carefully all the circumstances including:
   (i) The number in the party, and the age, experience, health, reliability and technical skills of each member;
   (ii) The nature of the country in which the activity is to take place;
   (iii) The weather conditions;
   (iv) The period of time required for completion of the activity allowing for delays;
   (v) His own personal experience in relation to the circumstances likely to be encountered.

(d) Generally observe every precaution that a reasonable and prudent parent would take for his family;

(iii) To ensure reliable communications in the event of an accident or emergency, a reliable person – "The Communicator" – must be appointed who can liaise, as appropriate, with the Police, rescue organisations, the "Host" and "Home" Scout authorities, and the next of kin. The "Communicator" should not be a close relative of any member of the party.

In the case of small parties of not more than eight members this responsibility may well be delegated to a Warden of a Hostel, Staff of a Mountain Rescue Post, local Police Station or similar establishment, but to ensure their effectiveness in the event of an accident or emergency they must have full details of route(s), timings, emergency equipment carried and an accurate list of names and addresses of appropriate home contacts of all personnel in the party.

In the case of a larger party the "Communicator" should not be actively engaged on that part of the expedition for which he is acting as the "Communicator".

40. Training, Accidents and Reports

(i) County and District Commissioners are responsible for ensuring that positive steps are taken for the education and training of Leaders on the content of these rules, the advice and guidance in *Safety on the Hills* and the responsibilities they have and must exercise when leading activities in potentially hazardous areas;

(ii) County and District Commissioners should strongly recommend and assist Leaders concerned with these activities to work towards the Mountain Leadership Certificate. County and District Mountaineering Advisers should be appointed;

(iii) (a) In the event of an accident or emergency requiring assistance the accident reporting procedure as prescribed in Appendix A in *Safety on the Hills* will be followed;

(b) In all other cases where the programme is impaired as a result of an incident which reflects upon the standards required by 'The Hill Safety Code' a similar report should be submitted to the Authorising Commissioner. This action should be taken to ensure that all possible assistance is given and to enable the Commissioner to decide whether any further action need be taken which may include a report to Headquarters.

41. Over-riding Controls

Notwithstanding these rules:–

(i) A Permission to Camp form must be submitted if the expedition is planned for five nights duration or longer.

(ii) The County or District Commissioner in any area where such activities take place – or their authorised representatives – have an over-riding authority:

(a) To ensure that all *Scouts* observe the requirements of paragraph 39(i) (see also *Policy, Organisation and Rules*, Appendix VI, paragraph 9(ix)),

(b) If in their view it is essential, in the interest of safety, to direct that any particular activities shall be stopped or cancelled.

APPENDIX A

ACCIDENT PROCEDURES AND REPORTS

Preamble

In the event of an accident or an emergency the immediate consideration is that of initiating adequate rescue arrangements and transmitting reliable information to those concerned.

Notwithstanding these primary considerations there exist two main areas of responsibility which have to be exercised both at the time of the occurrence and after the situation has been resolved. For ease of reference these are termed 'Immediate Action' and 'Follow-up Reports'.

A. Immediate Action

1. The Leader of the Party, or the Leader of the Section if for the specific activity the leadership of the party has been delegated as part of a training programme, and/or the communicator, must:
   (a) Alert and, as appropriate, arrange support for Rescue Facilities.
   (b) Advise the Host Scout Authority of the situation.
   (c) Advise the Home Scout Authorities and Group and maintain, as necessary, a periodic communications link providing full and clear reports relating to the accident or emergency and progress of rescue.
2. The Host Scout Authority should liaise with the Leader(s) concerned with the accident or emergency and:
   (a) Offer any support or guidance necessary
   (b) Ensure that the communications link with the Home Scout Authorities and Group has been established and is being maintained
   (c) Make an immediate assessment of the situa-

tion, possible causes, and extent of casualties and submit an interim report to Headquarters and if possible also to the Home County Commissioner(s) concerned.

3. The Home Scout Authorities should ensure that:
   (a) The communications link is being maintained.
   (b) Parents have, and continue, to receive full and clear reports relating to the accident and progress of the rescue.
   (c) As appropriate arrangements are made for assistance for the return of the party.
   (d) A brief interim report is prepared relating to the authorisation and training of the party concerned and is submitted to Headquarters and the Home County Commissioner(s) – as appropriate.

B. Follow-Up Reports

1. The Leader of the party involved, or a responsible member of it, should prepare a detailed report relating to the accident itself and submit it to his District and County Commissioner.
2. As soon as possible after the accident the Host Scout Authority should prepare a detailed report relating to the accident and rescue – incorporating information regarding rescue services and other assistance obtained – together with any observations relating to the effectiveness of the communications system and submit copies to both Headquarters and the Home County Commissioner(s). This report should *not* be concerned to apportion responsibility, but should aim to provide those essential facts which will help in providing further useful guidance relating to similar events.
3. The Home District Commissioner, in conjunction with the Leader of the party or other responsible person, will prepare a full confidential report relating to the authorisation, training, equipping, briefing and leadership of the party involved together with their observations relating to the sequence of the events and possible causes of the accident. This report will be submitted to the Home County Commissioner(s)

who will pass it to Headquarters accompanied by his own observations relating to the circumstances and the County support for education and training in respect of such activities and, as appropriate, any recommendations he intends to implement in the light of experience gained.

4. In the event of the normal channels of communication not being available or known, any stage in the procedure of investigation and report may be bypassed in the first instance provided steps are taken to transmit information to the appropriate quarters at the first opportunity.

Public Relations may not appear to be important at the time of an accident or incident, but inaccurate and misleading Press reports can cause a great deal of harm.

It is essential that a brief factual report be telephoned immediately to Scout Headquarters in London so that accurate information can be given to any Press enquiries. Leaders should telephone the Publicity Department, 01-834 6005. After hours: Harold Wyld, Barming Heath (Kent) 2244 or Jack Olden, 01-953 1393.

In Scotland: Office hours, Scottish Headquarters 031-226 7375. After hours: 031-332 5348.

APPENDIX B

MOUNTAIN LEADERSHIP CERTIFICATE SYLLABUS

The following gives the syllabus requirements of the Mountain Leadership Certificate, and highlights those skills that a Leader needs if he is to be able to give safe leadership in the mountains.

1. Map and Compass

(a) Map Scales.
(b) Conventional Signs.
(c) Map References – The Grid.
(d) Methods of showing relief.
(e) Contours – description of ground from information on the map.
(f) Topographical features.
(g) Measurement of distance.
(h) Calculation of speed of movement over varying terrain with and without loads – Naismith's Rule.
(i) Setting of the map – without compass.
(j) Navigation across country with map but no compass.
(k) Types of compass.
(l) Methods of obtaining Grid and Magnetic bearings.
(m) Plotting a compass course from the ground and from the map.
(n) Methods of obtaining a position fix by resection (Back-bearing).
(o) Navigation across country with map and compass especially in poor visibility (e.g. at night).
(p) Hints on natural wayfinding (e.g. use of sun or stars).
(q) Methods of teaching simple map and compass work to beginners.

2. Route Planning

(a) Choice of route.
(b) Preparation of route cards
    (i) – bearings,
    (ii) – distances covered,
    (iii) – time taken.
(c) Selection of camp sites.
(d) Expedition rationing.
(e) Escape routes.
(f) Bad weather alternatives.
(g) Sources of aid (telephones, mountain rescue posts, etc.).

3. Walking Skills

(a) Individual skills – pace, rhythm, foot placing, conservation of energy, balance and co-ordination.
(b) Party Skills – leader and tailman, psychology of the group, corporate strength.
(c) Party procedure on different terrain, e.g. scree, narrow ridge, steep broken slopes.

4. Personal Equipment

Personal equipment required for mountain expeditions, both high and low level and in *ALL* weather conditions. Information given should stress the effects of wind, temperature and humidity as well as providing information on design construction and types of material, care and maintenance of equipment.

5. Camping Equipment

(a) Knowledge of the use of different types and makes of:
    (i) tents,
    (ii) sleeping bags,
    (iii) stoves,
    (iv) rucsacs and other light-weight camping equipment.
(b) Knowledge of the principles of packing and loading personal and communal equipment.
(c) Care and maintenance of camping equipment.
(d) Knowledge of items required on given types of expedition, e.g. high level/low level, long duration/short duration camps.

6. Campcraft

(a) Camp organisation and siting.
(b) Tent organisation and siting.
(c) Camp daily routine.
(d) Hygiene in camp.
(e) 'The Country Code'.
(f) Camp foods and cooking.
(g) Use of mountain huts and bothies.

7. Security on Steep Ground

The small amount of rock climbing included in the course is not intended to train leaders as rock climbers. Its purpose is to familiarise candidates with elementary techniques, to enable them to appreciate the limits of what should be attempted by a party without rock climbing experience, to recognise difficulties and potential dangers of terrain and to give competent help in cases of emergency. Any safe method of rope management will be accepted at Assessment, but the method used and taught should involve the use of the rope alone. It is emphasised that the techniques advocated here are not necessarily those which would be suitable for rock climbing. The following points will be dealt with:

(a) Practice of movement on rock.
(b) Ropes and rope management, tying of figure-of-eight on the bight; waist belay with gloves, belaying and interchange of belay; moving together.
(c) Decision taking on steep, broken ground. Route selection, roping up, choice of belay, negotiating loose rock, etc.
(d) Use and limitations of hillwalking safety line (37 metres (120ft.) of No. 2 laid rope or 7mm or 9mm Kermantel rope).
(e) Use of rope as a handrail and for linking party together.
(f) Abseiling with safety rope.

8. River Crossing

When and when not to ford rivers, followed by practice in:

(a) methods of finding the best crossing points;
(b) methods of crossing with and without line;

(c) skills and safety precautions to be practised by the individual – method of progression, use of 'third leg', procedure with a pack, reduction of resistance or friction, danger from trees and snags.

9. Special Mountain Hazards

1. *Exposure*
   (a) An understanding of the causes of the condition known as Hypothermia (Exposure).
   (b) Recognition of the signs and symptoms exhibited by 'Exposure'.
   (c) Awareness of the basis for prevention of 'Exposure'.
   (d) Awareness of the methods for treatment of an 'Exposure' case
      (i) in the field,
      (ii) at base.

2. *Frostbite*
   An understanding of the condition, its signs, symptoms, prevention and treatment.

3. *Lightning*
   An understanding of the probable distribution of strikes on a mountain, and of the probable flow lines of resulting ground currents.

4. *Heat Exhaustion*
   An understanding of the condition, its signs, symptoms, prevention and treatment.

10. Weather

An elementary knowledge of weather, for example:

(a) interpretation of the weather map recognising:
   (i) areas of high pressure;
   (ii) air flows (e.g. northerly airstream);
   (iii) depressions and frontal systems;
   and weather normally associated with these.

(b) Major cloud and associated weather developments.

(c) Sources of information on weather, e.g. newspapers, radio/television broadcasts, R.A.F. stations.

11. Accident Procedure

Candidates must have practical ability and theoretical knowledge in depth of the following:

(a) procedure in the event of an accident;
(b) methods of search and evacuation;
(c) equipment contained in mountain rescue posts and boxes;
(d) improvised mountain rescue equipment – application and limitations;
rope seats;
rope stretchers;
sleds;
ski stretchers.

12. Details of Clubs, Organisations, etc.

(a) Details of organisations providing training in mountain activities.

(b) Details of clubs, etc., willing to accept young people as members.

(c) Guide books, etc.

13. Responsibilities of Party Leader, etc.

A thorough knowledge and awareness of the function and responsibilities of the party leader; see section 3 of this Appendix.

14. Additional Interests

A mountain leader should be knowledgeable in some or all of the following subjects:
Geology, flora and fauna, local history, history of mountaineering, photography, etc.